CHILDREN'S LIT.

SCURO

Wonders of zebras

DATE DUE			
JUL 09			
JUL 28			
MAY 02			
NOV 18			
MAY 6			
AUG 04			
OCT 24			

QL
737
.U62
S437

Missouri Western State College Library
St. Joseph, Missouri

843742

DODD, MEAD WONDERS BOOKS include WONDERS OF:

CATTLE. Scuro
CORALS AND CORAL REEFS. Jacobson and Franz
CROWS. Blassingame
DONKEYS. Lavine and Scuro
DRAFT HORSES. Lavine and Casey
DUST. McFall
EAGLE WORLD. Lavine
EGRETS, BITTERNS, AND HERONS. Blassingame
ELEPHANTS. Lavine and Scuro
FLIGHTLESS BIRDS. Lavine
FROGS AND TOADS. Blassingame
GEESE AND SWANS. Fegely
GOATS. Lavine and Scuro
HIPPOS. Lavine
LIONS. Schaller
MARSUPIALS. Lavine
MICE. Lavine
MULES. Lavine and Scuro
PEACOCKS. Lavine
PIGS. Lavine and Scuro
PONIES. Lavine and Casey
RACCOONS. Blassingame
RATTLESNAKES. Chace
RHINOS. Lavine
SEA HORSES. Brown
SEALS AND SEA LIONS. Brown
SHEEP. Lavine and Scuro
SNAILS AND SLUGS. Jacobson and Franz
SPONGES. Jacobson and Pang
TURTLE WORLD. Blassingame
WILD DUCKS. Fegely
WORLD OF BEARS. Bailey
WORLD OF HORSES. Lavine and Casey
ZEBRAS. Scuro

Wonders of

ILLUSTRATED WITH PHOTOGRAPHS AND OLD PRINTS

ZEBRAS

Vincent Scuro

Dodd, Mead & Company • New York

To all of my aunts, uncles, and cousins

ILLUSTRATIONS COURTESY OF: The Cincinnati Zoo, 16, 22 *bottom*, 44, 47, 61; The Dark Continent, Busch Gardens, Tampa, Florida, 12 *bottom*, 30, 57; Ted Lewin, *title page*; National Archives, 8, 12 *top*, 18, 22 *top*, 31, 33, 36 *bottom*, 39, 48, 56, 60; Pocono Wild Animal Farm, Mary B. Leister, 23 *top*; Vincent Scuro, 35; Six Flags Great Adventure, 45; SATOUR (South African Tourist Organization), 6, 14, 28, 36–37 *top*, 40, 41, 43, 50, 51; Tanzania Tourist Corporation Office, New York, 23 *bottom*, 53, 59.

Copyright © 1983 by Vincent Scuro
All rights reserved
No part of this book may be reproduced in any form
without permission in writing from the publisher
Distributed in Canada by McClelland and Stewart Limited, Toronto
Manufactured in the United States of America

1 2 3 4 5 6 7 8 9 10

Library of Congress Cataloging in Publication Data

Scuro, Vincent.
  Wonders of zebras.

  Includes index.
  Summary: Describes the evolution of zebras, their physical characteristics, behavior, natural habitat and the efforts of conservationists to help them survive in an increasingly hostile environment.
  1. Zebra—Juvenile literature. [1. Zebra] I. Title.
QL737.U62S38 1983   599.72′5   83-14053
ISBN 0-396-08227-0

Contents

1. Horses with Stripes? ... 7
   What is a Zebra? 9
   Early Ancestors 11
2. Zebras and Their Stripes ... 13
3. From A to Zebra ... 17
4. Meet the Zebras ... 21
   The Plains Zebra 21
   The Mountain Zebra 27
   Grevy's Zebra 29
   Domesticated Zebras 31
   Zebroids 32
5. Some Characteristics of Zebras ... 34
6. Life in the Wild ... 42
7. Zebras and Man ... 55
   Index ... 63

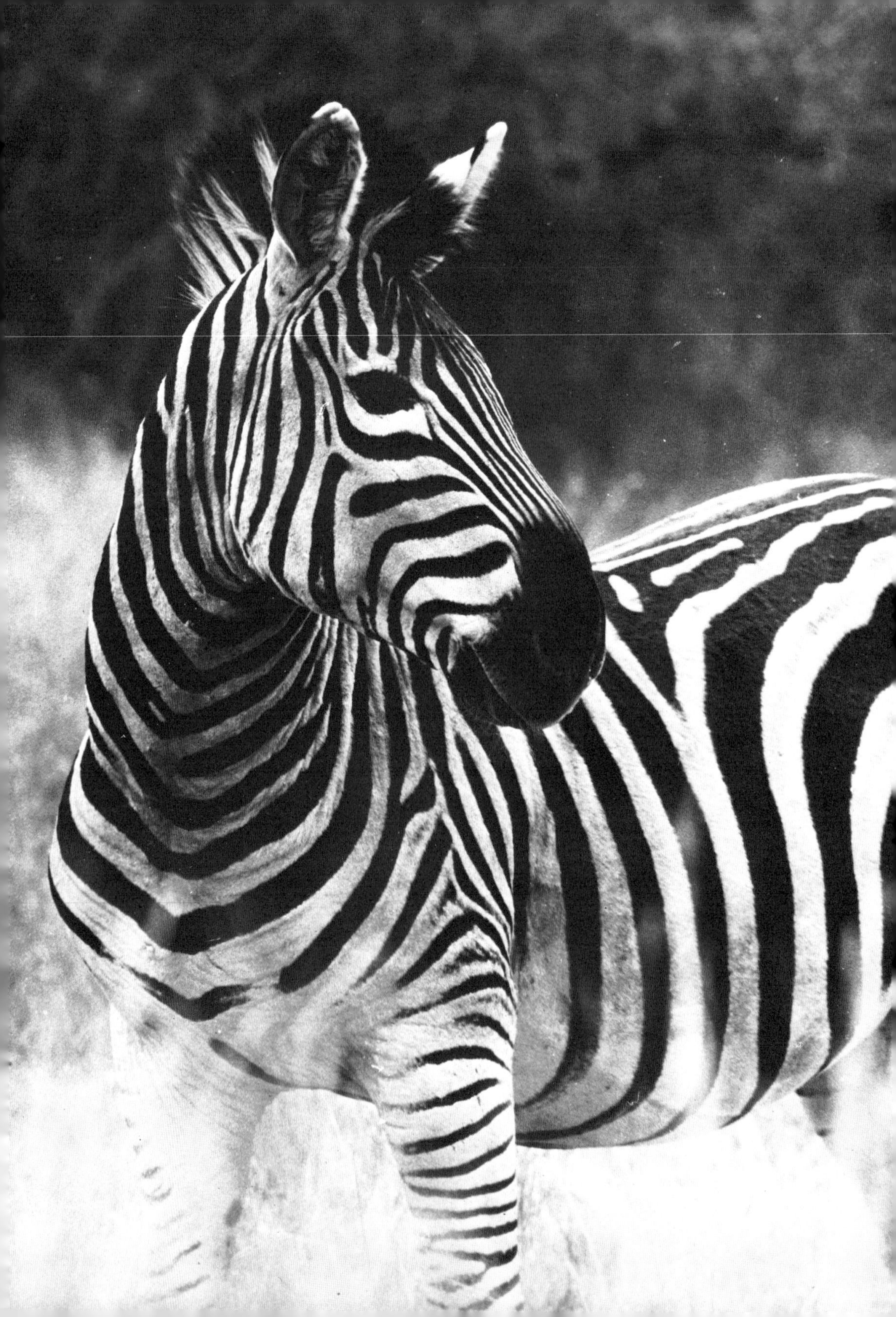

1
Horses with Stripes?

Accounts in modern books give the impression that zebras were discovered by Europeans on safari in Africa during the early nineteenth century. Yet ancient writings and tapestries reveal that zebras were known outside the Dark Continent over two thousand years ago.

It is worth mentioning that although the ancients knew *about* zebras, they really didn't know *what* they were. Seafaring Greeks who brought back tales of zebras from their trips to Africa saddled them with the misnomer *Hippotigris*—"horse-tiger." Early Romans who tamed these animals for use in their circuses described them as "the horses of the sun that resemble tigers." No doubt these and other references contributed to the myth that a zebra was a cross between a horse and a tiger!

Zoologists—scientists who study animals—have determined that zebras are not a combination of beasts. Nor are they "horses with stripes." Although the zebra is similar to the horse in basic form, there are a number of differences. Zebras are not as tall as

Zebras were a mystery to ancient peoples, who didn't know what they were. This beautiful plains zebra was photographed in South Africa.

Zebras differ from horses in many ways—note how the short mane on this plains zebra stands up. The mane of a horse is longer and flows.

most horses. The zebra's ears are typically longer than those of a horse, while the mane is shorter and more erect. The zebra's hoofs are smaller and narrower. Some zebras have folds of skin called a dewlap under the throat. Others lack chestnuts—the callus growths horses have on the inner leg above the knee and hock—on the hind legs. Furthermore, the world's horse population is largely domesticated, while the vast majority of zebras are wild.

What Is a Zebra?

A zebra is a member of the Equidae family and the *Equus* genus, in which horses, donkeys, and wild asses are included. Members of Equidae, commonly known as the horse family, are often referred to as equines.

Within *Equus*, the term zebra is applied to three subgroupings or species. The plains or common zebra (*Equus burchelli*) in-

Kiang, or Asiatic wild ass

Members of the Equidae family, clockwise from top left: African wild ass, Burchell's zebra, donkey, and Thoroughbred horse.

habits the Dark Continent's central and eastern flatlands. The mountain or true zebra (*Equus zebra*) roams the rocky stretches of land separating southern Africa's interior plateau from the coastal lowlands. Grevy's zebra (*Equus grevyi*), the so-called desert zebra, lives on the low hill country of eastern Africa. In some places, two or more species range over the same territory. Zebras are also found in zoos and nature reserves in virtually every part of the world.

The terminology of the horse is often used in describing individual zebras. Adult males and females are known as stallions and mares respectively. A young male is called a colt, while a young female is referred to as a filly. A baby of either sex is a foal; a one year old is a yearling.

Early Ancestors

The history of the evolution of zebras is not certain. Some authorities say today's zebras evolved separately from other equines, while there are those who believe modern zebras descended from striped ancestors. The most commonly accepted theory is that *Hyracotherium*, a small, stripeless, fox-like creature that wandered around the swamps and forests of North America some 40 to 60 million years ago, may have been the progenitor of all zebras. This animal is believed to have had a short neck, head, and face, as well as a flexible spine. Its body was supported by thin legs with four toes on the front feet and three on the rear. *Hyracotherium*'s diet consisted mainly of soft vegetation.

As the millenia passed, the descendants of this creature underwent numerous changes. The most obvious adaptation took place in the feet, which evolved from many toes on each foot to a single digit ending in a hoof. The remains of the side toes (called splint bones) are found on modern zebras.

It is believed that at the beginning of the Miocene era (some 25 million years ago) the early zebras traveled from North America across the land bridge that then connected Alaska and Asia. Because grass was so plentiful during this period, primitive zebras developed high-crowned, continuously growing grinding teeth that enabled them to feed on coarse vegetation. Additionally, their spines became somewhat rigid.

Fossils reveal that zebras resembling those existing today appeared in Europe about three million years ago. Some had teeth similar to those of modern zebras and may have had stripes on their bodies. It is generally thought that, about ten thousand to one million years ago, zebras drifted southward until they came upon the lush grasslands and sparsely wooded plains of the African continent. For some unknown reason, Europe's zebras disappeared during the same period. The zebras that went to Africa, however, throve.

Is a zebra white with black stripes . . .

or black with white stripes?

2
Zebras and Their Stripes

Is a zebra white with black stripes or black with white stripes? Be careful—there is no correct answer.

The degree of striping among zebras differs from one individual to another. A zebra's stripes may be thick, thin, numerous, sparse, or completely absent. Not all zebras are black and white. Depending on a number of factors (including age, sex, habitat, and even the time of year) a zebra may have black, white, brown, gray, yellow, red, or buff-colored stripes. There may be lighter bands (called shadow stripes) between the darker ones. In some cases, stripes are so faint the animal appears to be white. Zebras with spots are present in parts of Africa; they have stripes on the forequarters and dark circular patches on the hindquarters. Zebras with checkerboard markings have also been noted.

The stripe pattern on an individual zebra is as unique as a human's fingerprints. Variations in striping among zebras generally occur on the shoulders and hindquarters where the leg stripes meet those of the back. By studying photographs, scientists have disproven the common notion that all zebras look alike. It is also believed that zebras recognize each other by the patterns of their stripes.

The zebra's stripe pattern makes it difficult to tell where one animal ends and another begins.

A zebra's stripes serve a very important purpose. They create an optical illusion that provides protective camouflage. This effect, known as disruptive coloration, makes the animal's body difficult to distinguish from its surroundings. Viewed from a distance, a zebra seems to have no form. When two or more are standing close together, it is almost impossible to tell where one stops and another begins. Naturalists have noted that on a starlit night you can be standing close enough to a zebra to hear it breathing and still not be able to see it because the stripe pattern blends in with the shadowy lighting.

There is no question that stripes are a zebra's most prominent characteristic. Although tigers, antelope, skunks, and many other animals have stripes, nowhere in nature are stripes as pronounced as on zebras.

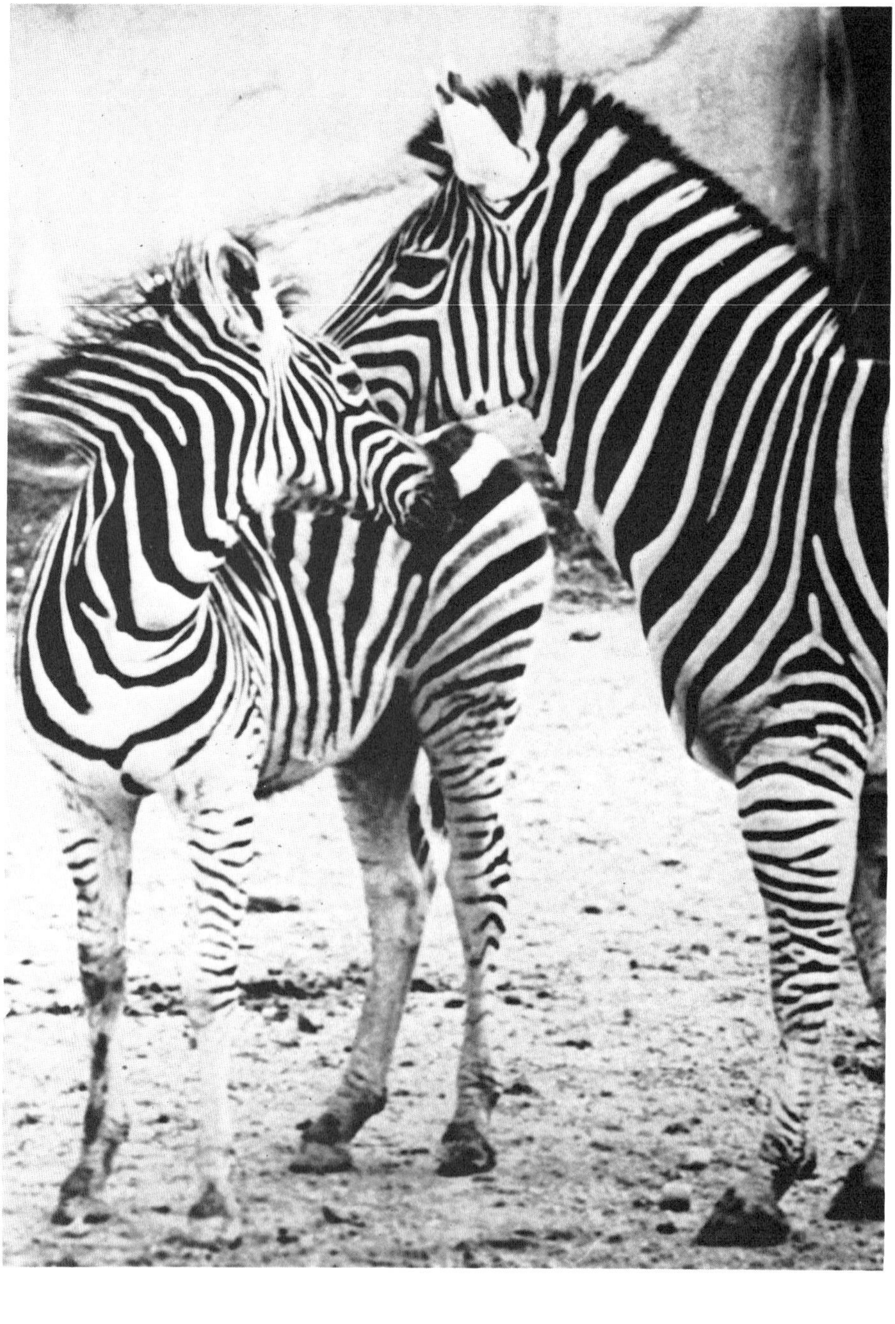

3
From A to Zebra

Lexicographers—compilers of dictionaries—are not certain about the origin of the word zebra. It may have come from an Amharic or Ethiopian expression signifying stripes. No one knows for sure.

Records indicate that the word zebra first gained popular usage in Europe about A.D. 1600. Common speech quickly adopted it as a synonym for stripes having a vertical or horizontal pattern. Since a zebra's markings may run in different directions on the various parts of its body, the term has also been applied to other types of stripes.

This four-legged equine does not have exclusive rights to the usage of its name, however. There are other zebras in nature, including a butterfly, a finch, and a fish. All have distinctive stripe patterns. Zebra wood, which is found in tropical America, is known for its hardness as well as its stripes. The zebra-plant of Brazil has yellow-green and olive-green stripes on its leaves. Elsewhere, zebra-like stripes are found on the uniforms worn by

A zebra's stripes create a pattern that is dizzying to the eyes of an observer.

All zebras do not look alike.

Illustration from a children's book shows a zebra in an animal parade.

referees of some sports. They are also present on the signs at dangerous curves on America's roadways.

Zebras are mentioned in the lore of some cultures. According to Watusi legend, zebras are the allies of elephants and rhinos in the war for grazing rights against antelope, gnu, and giraffes. Although the Old Testament does not refer to zebras by name, paintings of Noah's Ark typically show a pair of zebras walking immediately behind two elephants.

Our common speech has been enriched by sayings involving zebras. When asked an obvious question, some people reply, "Do zebras have stripes?" The maxim "A zebra can't change its stripes" is usually applied to a person who has little hope of altering the way he behaves. "A horse of another color," once used to describe zebras, now refers to anything unique or different.

Americans have found a number of useful ways to employ zebras. Stores specializing in a variety of goods advertise that they have everything from "A to Zebra." Children learn the

Z was a zebra,
    All striped white and black;
    And if he were tame,
    You might ride on his back.

Edward Lear used a zebra in one of his nonsense alphabets.

alphabet by associating the letter Z with a picture of this animal. In schoolyards, zebras provide laughter, courtesy of jokes that have been around for a long time: To "stop a zebra from charging" simply "take away its credit card." And everyone knows the answer to the question: "What is black and white and red all over?"

Why, an embarrassed zebra, of course!

4
Meet the Zebras

The Plains Zebra

The plains zebra holds the distinction of being the only wild equine still found in great numbers. In Tanzania's Serengeti Plain, a vast area teeming with wildlife, there are places where plains zebras cover the landscape for as far as the eye can see. Records show that 150,000 have been observed in a single location. Some herds average about ten thousand animals. Others are smaller.

Each of the three living subspecies of plains zebra (called *bontequagga* by native Africans) has a horselike body and head. They also have a black muzzle and a tail with a fairly long tassle. Standing from 50 to 64 inches high at the shoulder, these animals weigh from 500 to 600 pounds.

Arrangement of stripes and geographical location assist in identifying the different plains zebras. The Damara or Chapman's zebra (*Equus burchelli antiquorum*) has a highly irregular stripe pattern typified by light-brown shadow stripes on the hindquarters. Dark and light bands reach to but are often absent below the knees. An inhabitant of the borderlands separating Angola and South-West Africa, this subspecies also ranges

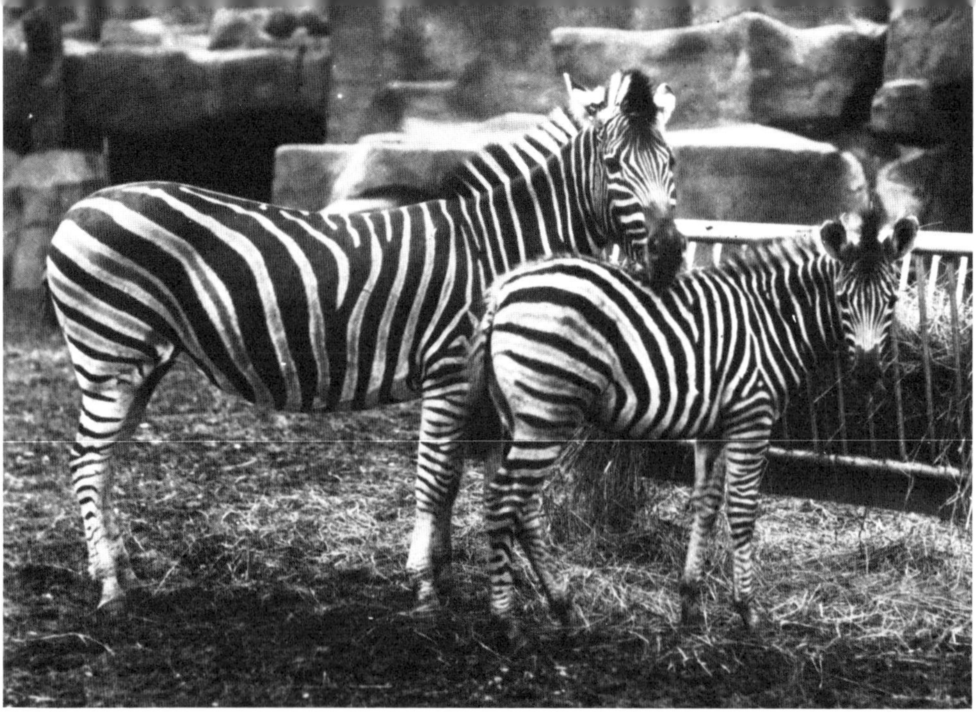

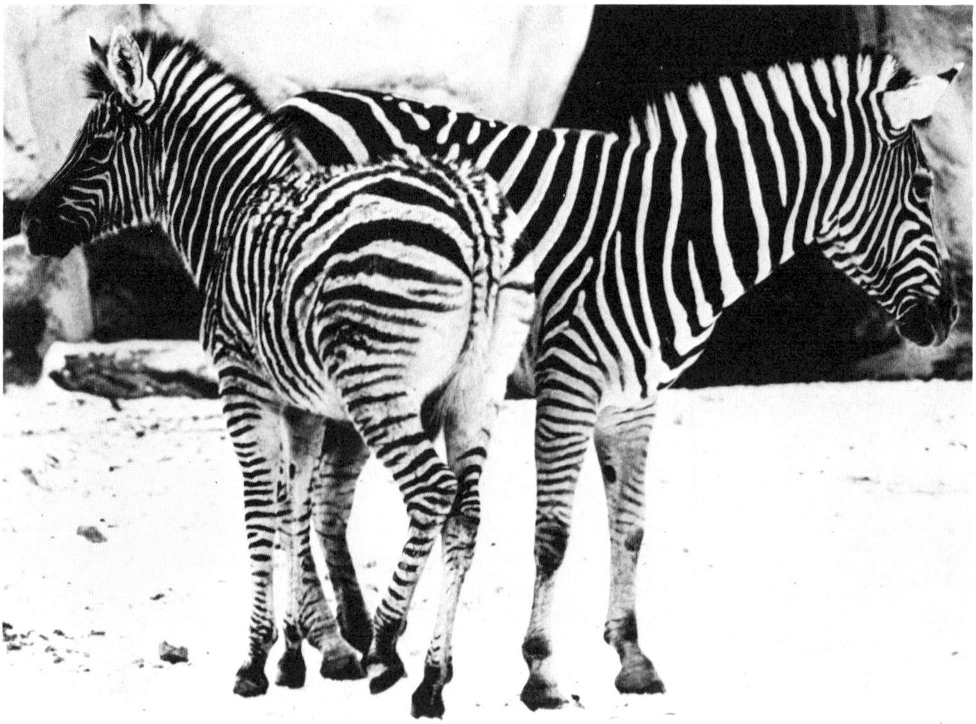

Plains zebras—

Left top: *Chapman's zebras at the Detroit Zoo, and,* left below: *at the Cincinnati Zoo. Note the shadow stripes.*

Right: *Grant's zebras at the Pocono Wild Animal Farm, Pennsylvania.*

Left: *A Grant's zebra, photographed in Tanzania.*

throughout South Africa, Botswanna, and Rhodesia as far north as the Zambesi River.

Grant's or Boehm's zebra (*Equus burchelli boehmi*) has widely spaced stripes all over its body, including the area below the knees. *Boehmi* is often regarded as an east African subspecies, roaming from Tanzania and Kenya to Ethiopia and the southern Sudan. It is the smallest of the plains zebras.

Selous' zebra (*Equus burchelli selousi*) is an elusive animal that inhabits the ranges from Victoria Falls through eastern Zambia and southern Malawi. *Selousi*'s stripes are narrower, more numerous, and closer together than its other plains relatives.

For many years, "Burchell" was the common name applied to

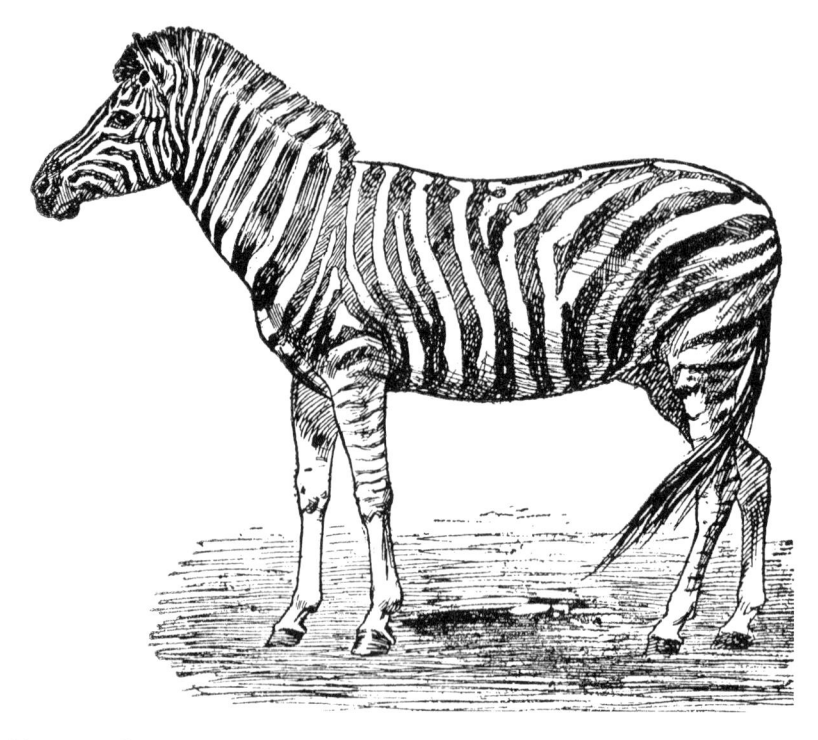

Old print of plains zebra, referred to as "Burchell's." The true Burchell's zebra is extinct.

Old print of quagga, now extinct

all plains zebras. Only recently has a distinction been made between the true Burchell's zebra (*Equus burchelli burchelli*), which is now extinct, and the other plains varieties.

Named after William John Burchell (1782-1863), an English naturalist who first described it in the journal of his African explorations from 1811-12, the true Burchell's zebra had reddish-brown and white stripes over most of its body with shadow stripes between the broad bands on its head, neck, and hindquarters. Its limbs were white.

Although Burchell's zebras were popular in European zoos during the late nineteenth century, conditions in captivity were not conducive to reproduction. Meanwhile, colonists in Africa were wiping out whole herds to feed their farm workers. By 1910, the entire wild population was gone. The last Burchell's zebra died in a Berlin zoo eight years later.

Most zoologists treat another plains zebra, the quagga (*Equus quagga quagga*), as a distinct species. Some categorize this animal as a variety of *Equus burchelli*. Others say the different subspecies of plains zebra are actually subspecies of *quagga*. In any case, the debate is academic. The quagga has been extinct for over a hundred years.

The quagga was a very useful creature that could be captured and domesticated with relative ease. South African farmers, who admired their courage, often kept one or two to protect livestock from wild dogs and hyenas. A pair imported to London during the early 1800's were trained to pull a coach.

The quagga was heavily built, in many ways resembling a medium-sized donkey. Standing from 51 to 57 inches high at the shoulder, it had brown and white stripes on its head, neck, and foreparts. These markings faded on the flanks to a color ranging from pale red or yellowish-brown to dark brown. Its legs and belly were completely white.

A herd of quaggas was an impressive sight to see. They trotted from place to place in single file, crying a shrill, barking neigh—*Kwa-ha! Kwa-ha!*—from which their name is derived. Unfortunately, about 1820, greedy hunters discovered that quaggas were worth more dead than alive. In South Africa, thousands and thousands were shot for meat to feed the colonists. Quagga skins were tanned for leather, and dried hides served as grain sacks. When a lucrative market developed for striped harnesses, the quagga was doomed.

Hunting the quagga required no skill. It was simple, brutal slaughter. Heavily armed men in wagon trains traveled out to the countryside and shot every one they saw. Quaggas were easy targets. Their slow-moving single file enabled even the most inept marksman to bring them down.

The last free-roaming quagga was killed in 1878. Ironically, no one had realized the species was in danger of extinction until it was too late.

In 1883, a European zookeeper wired his African game supplier to send a quagga to replace one that had died.

The chilling reply came back: "But there aren't any more."

The Mountain Zebra

First described by Linnaeus in 1758, the mountain zebra has been characterized by tourists as a stocky little animal. Indeed, this zebra, known to South Africans as the *berkwagga*, has a strong, well-proportioned body with short wiry legs. It is easily distinguished from the plains zebras by a dewlap on the throat, a brown muzzle, ears that are long and tapered, and the lack of shadow stripes on the hindquarters. Transverse stripes across the

Old print shows the true or mountain zebra.

One of the few remaining mountain zebras (Cape subspecies), photographed in Mountain Zebra National Park, South Africa

rump form a gridiron pattern. The legs are closely banded down to the hoofs. The tail is scantily haired, having a short tuft.

Herds of mountain zebras are small, averaging about six animals. When food is plentiful, they assemble in larger numbers. Scientists have noted that mountain zebras are creatures of habit, traveling over the same trails time and time again. They are also considered to be excellent climbers and have been observed moving up and down rocky hills in single file.

Two subspecies of mountain zebra have been noted. The Cape variety (*Equus zebra zebra*) has stripes over every part of its body except the stomach and inner thighs. Standing 48 inches high at the shoulder, this is the smallest of all zebras.

During the early 1900's, excessive hunting and human expansion drove the Cape mountain zebra to the brink of extinction. By

1913, there were only twenty-seven specimens left in the world. These were in South Africa. Three years later, the outlook was so bleak that encyclopedias began referring to this subspecies in the past tense. By then it was clear that unless special measures were taken, the Cape mountain zebra was doomed.

In 1937, the National Parks Board of South Africa purchased a hilly farm named Babylons Toren and established Mountain Zebra National Park as a sanctuary dedicated to the preservation of a specific animal. Under this special protection, the Cape variety has been saved. As of 1983, over two hundred thrive there; another forty roam Karoo National Park near Beaufort West. Smaller herds have been established in other parts of the country.

Hartmann's mountain zebra (*Equus zebra hartmannae*) is considered to be a relative of the Cape subspecies because it is similar in basic physical form. The main difference is that the Hartmann's variety is slightly taller and has stripes that are narrower and closer together.

This zebra once existed in great numbers in South-West Africa, from the arid mountains on the western range of the Namib Desert to the coastal flatlands. Today, the population is dwindling rapidly due to vanishing rangeland and poaching. There are now only about seven thousand free-roaming Hartmann's mountain zebras. Most of these live within thirty miles of the ocean.

Grevy's Zebra

Although no scientific description of *Equus grevyi* existed until 1882, this was probably the first zebra known to western civilization. Scenes of the Nativity from the early centuries sometimes included a Grevy's zebra instead of a donkey. African tribes have always prized *grevyi*. The emperors of Ethiopia were so impressed with this animal that they often gave one as a gift to

Grevy's zebras have large, conical ears. These were photographed at Busch Gardens, Florida.

European rulers. Indeed, Grevy's zebra derives its name from President Jules Grévy of France who received a fine specimen from Menelik I in 1880.

Grevy's zebra is truly a magnificent animal. It has been described as having the size and stature of a medium-sized horse with the ears and voice of a donkey. The largest of all zebras, *grevyi* stands a little over five feet at the shoulder. Its ears, which are long, conical, and rounded at the top, are situated on a thick, ponderous head.

Brilliant bands of dark and light arranged in a striking pattern distinguish this zebra from its mountain and plains cousins. Its stripes are numerous and narrow, virtually covering the animal from head to hoof. On the haunches, black stripes from the flanks and hindlegs bend toward the rump and join up. A single stripe bisects the hindquarters, running up the back to the peak of the mane. The belly is unstriped.

Grevy's zebra inhabits the semidesert and hills of northern Kenya, southern and eastern Ethiopia, and western Somaliland. Over the years, the African *grevyi* population has been reduced considerably through human thoughtlessness and greed. Fortunately, this species is in no danger of extinction. Grevy's zebra reproduces well in captivity and thrives in many different climates.

Domesticated Zebras

Textbooks written in the 1920's note that zebras "seem incapable of domestication." Although this assertion is not accurate in all cases, there is a great deal of truth to it. Zebras have never taken to being tamed. However, some individuals have been taught to work in harness. Others have been used for entertainment purposes in circuses.

During the late 1800's, the Zeederberg Mail Coach Company of South Africa attempted to use zebras to pull coaches loaded

Some zebras have been domesticated. A pair of plains zebras pulling a milk wagon in St. Louis, about 1929.

with prospectors and gold in and out of mining areas. Unfortunately, the zebras did not have enough stamina to make the trips in a timely manner, and this practice was discontinued. Had it worked, transportation companies like the Zeederberg outfit would have overcome the problem of losing their horses and mules to *nagana*, a form of insect-transmitted sleeping sickness that afflicts livestock and humans—but not zebras.

About the same time, Russia, France, and other countries established large-scale domestication programs in Africa. Soon they discovered that the time and expense involved in capturing and training large numbers of zebras was not worth the effort because no consistent results could be achieved. Thus, the hope of using the vast herds of African zebras as a steady supply of animals for transportation in tropical regions was abandoned.

Zebroids

The different zebra species seldom interbreed in the wild but they have been mated in captivity. Similarly, zebras have no natural inclination to mate with other equines. Man has succeeded in breeding them with horses and donkeys. This is usually accomplished by forcing a zebra to associate only with members of the other species.

The product of crossing a zebra with a horse is called a zebrule or horse-zebroid. The terms zebrass, zedonk, and donkey-zebroid are used to describe the offspring of a zebra and a donkey.

Most zebroids resemble their dams (mothers) more than their sires (fathers). A certain degree of striping is always present. Incidentally, there is no scientific evidence to support the superstitious belief that if a mare or a jenny (female donkey) is mated to a zebra stallion, all future offspring of that mare or jenny will be striped!

Some zebroids are easily managed and serve well as beasts of

This baby zebroid, whose father is a huge wild ass, was born in the Berlin Zoo. Its mother is a plains zebra. The legs of this little creature are zebralike, but otherwise it looks like a wild ass.

burden. Others are so shy they are unsuitable for any type of work. Many are bad tempered, easily panicked, and apt to kick anything in sight! Since the disposition of a zebra-hybrid is usually unpredictable and because they are unable to reproduce, large-scale production of zebroids has been impractical.

5
Some Characteristics of Zebras

Nineteenth-century English naturalist Charles Darwin theorized that all creatures struggle for their existence. Those that are favorably adapted to their surroundings, said Darwin, survive in greater numbers and produce more offspring than those that are not. When applied to zebras, this theory is fairly accurate. Indeed, few animals are better adapted to life in the rugged mountains, vast desert plains, and seemingly endless grasslands of Africa than zebras.

There are certain characteristics that are common to all zebras. Thus, except where noted, the features described in the pages that follow apply equally to the three species.

Like horses, donkeys, and wild asses, a zebra is perfectly designed for efficiency in running. Its body is harmoniously proportioned, containing a strong heart and lungs. It has neat feet and powerful hindquarters. The upper limbs are short and well muscled, providing power for motion. The lower limbs are long, slender, and relatively unmuscled. Only one digit on each foot (a fully developed middle toe surrounded by a hoof) touches the ground. The joints, ligaments, and tendons act as shock absorbers, cushioning the force of each step.

Zebras are designed for efficiency in running. Note the long, slender lower limbs of this plains zebra.

It has been said that a zebra is born to run because its efficient running motion is instinctive. At a gallop, this animal thrusts off the ground with its hindlegs, swinging the body forward by pivoting over the front legs. A zebra can also walk, canter, or trot.

Speed, agility, and endurance are essential to survival in the wild. Zebras possess all three. Scientists have clocked them at sixty miles per hour for distances of a few hundred yards. They can also average speeds of thirty to forty miles per hour for up to

Zebras can run at incredible speeds for short distances.

Were this mother and baby startled by the person who took the photograph? Note the ears straining forward, a sign of fear.

fifteen miles. Even on the darkest night, a herd of these animals can run at twenty-five miles per hour and still stay close together without tripping over each other. Zebras are capable of executing sharp turns at high speed with relative ease.

A zebra's legs and hoofs carry it away from danger and serve as weapons in a fight. If they are injured—legs and hoofs are extremely delicate—a zebra faces certain death.

A zebra's eyes are set high on the sides of the head. Like all side-eyed animals, it has trouble judging distances. Zebras can see the details of objects that are far away much better than a man can. They also have excellent nighttime vision.

A sharp sense of smell aids in distinguishing friend from foe and helps the mares identify their foals. Zebras also rely on their good hearing to warn them of approaching danger. In addition to collecting sounds, the ears provide to observers, as well as to other zebras, an indication of the individual's emotional state. Erect ears mean all is well. Ears straining forward are a sign of fear. If a zebra pulls its ears back, watch out! It's angry about something.

The voices of zebras differ according to species. A plains zebra makes a sound like a barking dog. The Grevy's species speaks with a noise that resembles a hoarse grunt followed by a shrill whistle. A mountain zebra's voice is a low, soft whinny—quite unlike the raucous calls of its zebrine relatives.

Like most animals, zebras use their voices to communicate with each other. Several different calls have been recorded, including a greeting, two distinct alarms, two exclamations of pain, one of well-being, and a plaintive cry for help from foals. It is believed that one zebra can recognize another by the sound of its voice.

A zebra's mouth has soft, flexible lips that are used to gather food. The lips also help in chewing, although most of this is done by the teeth. During maturity there may be thirty-six to forty teeth, depending on the individual's age. The incisors are for biting off food; the molars grind and crush it. High-crowned cheek teeth with hard foldings enable the zebra to dine on coarse fodder. Generally, canine teeth are not present.

When it comes to eating, the zebra is neither finicky nor indiscriminate. It can thrive in places that will not support most livestock, including horses and donkeys. In the wild, a zebra's diet consists of the vegetation in season in a particular locale. During the spring, plains and mountain zebras graze on tender short grasses that are rich in protein. When the hot dry weather comes, tall grasses high in cellulose are eaten. Grevy's zebras browse on shrubs, herbs, and bulbs.

In captivity, zebras usually follow a food management program similar to that of domestic equines. Some eat grass and about twenty pounds of timothy hay per day. Their diet also includes vegetables (especially corn and carrots in cold climates) and vitamin supplements. Salt in block form is available at all times.

The old adage about leading a horse to water also applies to zebras. They cannot be forced to drink. Nevertheless, all zebras need water. The individual requirement varies from one species to another. Plains and Grevy's zebras must have water every thirty-six hours. The mountain species can survive by drinking

In captivity, zebras have salt available in block form.

only once in three or four days. Hartmann's mountain zebras are particularly adept at finding water. They can sniff out underground pools, dig a three-foot hole, and uncover a fresh supply.

To relieve the itching and scaling of dry skin brought on by too much sun and hot winds, zebras scratch. They delight in this activity because it keeps them well groomed.

Zebras love to rub against boulders, trees, stumps, even other zebras. They also groom themselves by nibbling each other on the neck and shoulders. For itches in hard to reach places, zebras roll on the ground. This covers them with a layer of dirt or mud that protects their coats from the searing heat and brutal winds of the African wilds. Zebras are protected from insects by a variety of birds called tick birds. These eat the tiny pests that burrow into animal hides.

The seemingly placid behavior of zebras has convinced many people that they are cowardly animals. Evidence indicates this is totally false. When attacked, a zebra will defend itself fero-

Three plains zebras enjoying a drink

A pair of zebras rubbing cheek to cheek

ciously, biting and kicking with teeth and hoofs. Contrary to popular belief, zebras do not panic at the sight of fire and do not flee at the sound of a lion's roar. Nor do they fear man. If provoked, a zebra will charge a car or jeep. Stories are told of poachers who have been stomped to death or maimed by irate mares reacting to the murder of their foals.

Although a variety of personality types have been observed among individual zebras, the plains, mountain, and Grevy's species can best be described as wary, savage, and indifferent, respectively. While scientists are unable to agree on why the different zebras behave the way they do, they do concur on one thing—*all* zebras can be unpredictable.

6
Life in the Wild

From birth to death, a zebra's life in Africa's savage wilderness is filled with danger. Disease, drought, and starvation threaten its existence. Marauding predators lurk at every turn. In this hostile environment, the slow, the weak, and the careless die.

Since there is safety in numbers, zebras congregate in herds. Other reasons for forming herds include breeding, locating food, or simply enjoying each other's company.

Much has been written about the migrations of plains zebras. Observations indicate that these animals travel hundreds of miles every year. Field naturalists believe this movement is linked to survival instincts, especially the need to find food and water.

In Africa, as in other parts of the world, changes in the weather greatly alter the environment. During the early months of the year, huge numbers of plains zebras congregate in the bushland. In the dry season, smaller herds break away to search for permanent grass near water holes and rivers. When the rains come, the great herds form again to dine on the fresh growth of tender short grasses.

Grevy's zebras also migrate with the seasonal changes but cover a much smaller amount of territory. The movement of

Zebras form herds to enjoy each other's company. This one is in Kruger National Park, South Africa.

mountain zebras is limited largely to the parks and reserves they inhabit, but it, too, is tied to the search for food and water.

The social organization of zebra herds varies from one species to another. Plains herds are made up of a number of smaller groups, each with its own distinct identity. A dominant stallion and five or six mares with young comprise a family. This group is close knit, staying together throughout the year. When a family travels, the mares lead the youngsters while the stallion brings up the rear. Other groups within a plains zebra herd include older stallions that live alone and young males that congregate in "bachelor" groups of ten to fifteen. Generally, bachelor stallions live together until they are ready to start their own families.

The organization of mountain zebra herds is similar to that of the plains species but on a much smaller scale. Here, families consist of a stallion and one or two mares with their young. Bachelor groups are present but have no more than two or three members. Similarly, there are older stallions that live a solitary life, joining the others only when it is time to eat or drink.

Herds of Grevy's zebras are organized differently. There are stallion groups, mare groups (with or without foals), and groups of stallions and mares. None have permanent membership. The dominant stallion of a particular herd patrols a mile-wide strip of land he has claimed for himself and his females. Other males are tolerated within this area unless they approach one of his mares.

Some zebras would rather be alone.

Right: *A beautiful Grevy's zebra foal*

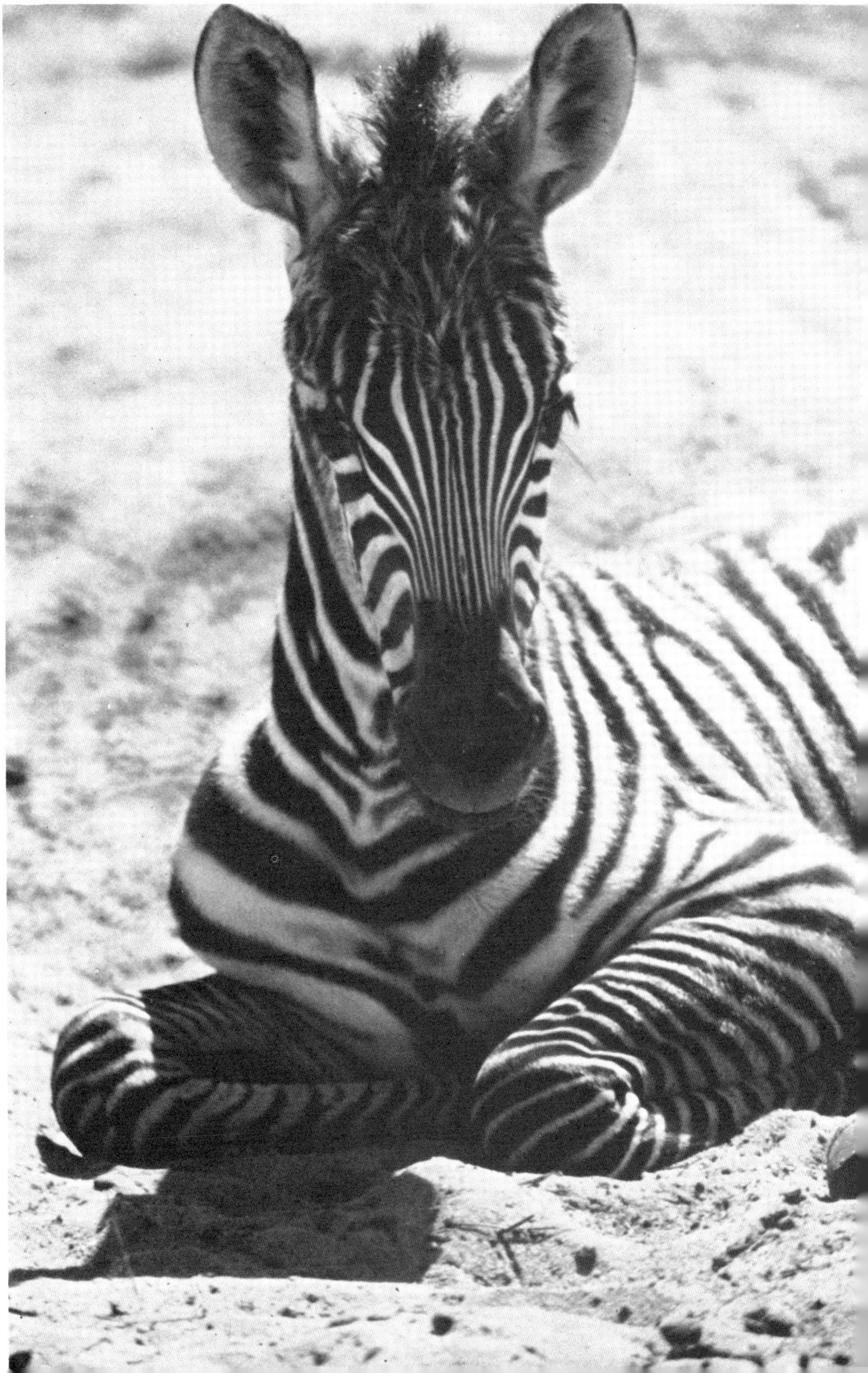

In all zebra herds, competition between stallions is ferocious. Fights break out frequently. When one male challenges another, it is usually over food, territory, or the right to mate with a female. The strongest stallion seldom seeks a fight. Instead, he waits to be challenged. When a challenger approaches, he lays back his ears, snorts wildly, and prepares for combat. In most cases, this display of anger is sufficient to discourage an adversary, which may simply turn and run. If a fight does take place, there is a lot of pounding on the ground, neck-wrestling, biting, and kicking. Contrary to popular belief, zebras seldom attack each other with their front hoofs. The risk of injury is too great. Nor do they fight to the death. Generally, the weaker zebra gives up and gallops away.

Occasionally, a stallion will leave his family or the land he has claimed to search for food and water. His females, of course, have no way of knowing when or even if he'll return. They attempt to remain faithful to him, resisting advances of unfamiliar stallions, who are rebuked with a swift kick! But if, after a few days, the original stallion doesn't come back, the mares recognize the strongest and most determined suitor as their new stud. If the original stallion does return, the new one either leaves or fights for the right to stay and breed.

Zebras reproduce at a relatively slow rate. Most mares give birth every three years, beginning at age two. Gestation lasts from eleven to thirteen months and results in a single offspring. Twin births are extremely rare.

Shortly before the female foals, she searches for a quiet, private place away from the herd. Most mares move to areas where the grass is not too tall, and they deliver their foals alone.

A newborn zebra usually has a shaggy coat of brown and white or buff-colored stripes. Most are short bodied and long legged, resembling the foals of domestic horses.

A newborn zebra foal usually can walk and run an hour after birth.

Baby zebras are fascinating creatures to observe. A foal usually stands on wobbly legs a few minutes after it is born. But it can run an hour later. As they trot back to the safety of the herd, foals stay close to their mothers' flanks.

Like all newborns, baby zebras need lots of nourishment. Colostrum, the first food a foal receives from its mother's mammary glands, is rich in protein. It also contains antibodies which

The muscles of an adult zebra automatically support its body at all times, enabling the animal to relax and sleep in an upright position.

give the youngster immunity to many diseases. Gradually, foals are weaned from their mothers' milk. Then they eat the available vegetation.

During the first few weeks of life, foals sleep on the ground. Their mothers stand nearby dozing. The mothers will wake their youngsters at the slightest danger and run with them if necessary. Incidentally, the muscles of an adult zebra automatically support its body at all times, enabling the animal to relax and sleep in an upright position.

Foals love to play. One way they have fun is by frolicking with members of neighboring families. They also enjoy racing or playing tag with each other. These activities are important since they help develop speed, strength, reflexes, and agility, which can mean the difference between life and death in an emergency. Adult zebras play-fight with their offspring to prepare them for possible confrontations with predators or other zebras. Adults also play for the sheer joy of it. Their favorite pastime is circling a rhino at high speed, which is great fun for the zebras but drives the rhino crazy!

After several years of growing up, young zebras move away from their families. At two years of age, fillies join other families or become members of mare groups. At about the same age, a colt starts running with bachelor groups. By the time he is five or six years old, he tries to corral a few young mares to start his own family or challenges other zebras for their territory. At about the same age, a zebra assumes another important responsibility—defense of the herd.

In the wild there are hunters and the hunted; predators and prey. Since zebras do not kill other animals for food and are sought by a variety of predators, they are classified as prey.

Yet zebras are not an easy kill, probably because they take numerous precautions to protect themselves. If two zebras are standing side by side in an open field, they usually face in opposite directions, each keeping a lookout for potential attackers. Zebras rarely rest anywhere there is tall grass that could conceal an enemy. When they stop to eat, a sentry is posted. At night, stallions stand guard because an assault is most likely to come after dark. If an attack occurs, the stallions stay behind to face their aggressors while the rest of the herd flees for safety.

The deep sense of loyalty among members of zebra herds also

When zebras stop at a water hole in an open area, one usually stands guard while the others drink.

helps them survive the dangers of the wild. If a mare and her foal are attacked, a call for help brings five or six stallions racing to the rescue. When a zebra is injured or crippled and can no longer keep pace with the herd, the others slow down. Nor are the aged cast aside. Old zebras are brought food, which the other members carry in their mouths. They are also helped along and protected.

Lions are perhaps the greatest wild enemy of zebras. However, the toll taken by these big cats is greatly exaggerated. Lions kill only about two percent of all zebras each year, and these are usually the weak and the sick.

As noted, zebras do not always run at the sound of a lion's roar. Nevertheless, they are extremely wary of this enemy. The sighting of a lone lion causes considerable tension. However, this uneasiness is hardly noticeable. The zebras continue to graze quietly, always keeping the predator in view. If the lion approaches or makes any threatening motion, a signal is passed from one zebra to another and, in a split second, the entire herd takes off in all directions "with tails flying, heads held high, and clouds of dust." Incidentally, scientists have been unable to determine the exact nature of this signal, even with the aid of slow-motion photography and sensitive sound detection equipment.

If more than one lion attacks a herd, zebras use a different

Zebras associate with giraffes—and run with them when danger approaches.

defensive tactic. They huddle together, stallions protecting the sides and rear. Any lion that penetrates the stallions must contend with the mares, who defend their foals and themselves to the death.

Occasionally, a lion tries to make a meal of a lone stallion. To accomplish this, it must surprise its quarry with a swift kill, which is not as simple as it sounds. Zebras that live alone are always on guard. Whenever they see, smell, or hear a lion, they take off in the opposite direction. Even if a lion is cunning enough to sneak up unnoticed, it must catch its prey in the first hundred yards of the chase. A zebra can easily outrun a lion over a long distance. Furthermore, a stallion is a deadly adversary when cornered. He can stomp a lion to death, or crush its vital organs with a well-placed kick.

Lions are not the only wild enemies of zebras. In some parts of Africa, crocodiles have been known to attack zebras at water

Old print from a nineteenth-century geography book shows a lion, lioness, and young. Lions are the wild zebra's great enemy.

Zebras get along well with antelope.

holes. However, these reptiles are only successful if their quarry is caught off guard. Packs of wild dogs and hyenas prey on any member of a herd that straggles behind, but when they attack a herd head on, they are easily driven off by one or two stallions.

Most zoologists say zebras mingle well with other nonpredators. Others think they simply tolerate them. Many seem to agree that zebras never lower their guard, even when associating with creatures that represent no threat to their safety. Zebras may drink with gnu or giraffes, but that doesn't mean they trust them. Nevertheless, zebras derive a certain amount of security by socializing with these animals. Giraffes (with their long necks and elevated view) and gnu (with their well-deserved reputation for skittishness) provide zebras with an early warning of approaching danger.

Contrary to legend, zebras seem to have a special affection for antelope. Not only do they graze with these creatures but stories are told of stallions saving does (female antelope) and their young from attacks by wild dogs and hyenas.

7
Zebras and Man

Man represents the most urgent threat to the survival of zebras in their natural habitat. For centuries, native Africans have hunted zebras, using their skins for clothing and their flesh for food. The meat of a zebra is said to resemble beef, though it is more delicate in flavor.

In certain tribes, some members dress up as lions while others paint their bodies with stripes, acting out the roles of predator and prey. This ritual is believed to ensure a successful hunt. Actually, the number of zebras killed by native Africans has very little impact on the total zebra population. The greatest losses are the result of modern man's greed.

A zebra's handsome hide offers temptation to professional poachers who use illegal, merciless hunting methods that cause a cruel death. Motivated by the demand for striped shoes, handbags, coasters, phone book covers, and wall hangings, these vicious individuals profit while thousands of zebras die needlessly. Without this lucrative market, the slaughter would probably stop.

Governments throughout the world are trying to prevent this illegal killing, with little success. It is extremely difficult to stop

Foals are short bodied and long legged. A Grevy's zebra.

poachers. Records show that in a recent year, one poacher destroyed four thousand zebras without being caught.

In some countries, licensed hunters are permitted to shoot zebras for "sport." Fortunately, this type of slaughter is strictly controlled.

A serious threat to the survival of free-roaming zebras comes from the spread of modern civilization into their ranges. Each year, thousands of acres are plowed under for farming or fenced in for ranching. In some areas, zebras compete with livestock for scarce water and sparse vegetation. Elsewhere, they have been driven from their original habitats and forced into highly undesirable areas.

Conservationists clamor for the preservation of the land where zebras and other animals have lived for thousands of years. Their appeals have not gone unnoticed.

In many, but not all, African countries the attitude toward nature is changing. Where exploitation was once encouraged, free-roaming animals are now treasured as valuable natural re-

Attendants at the Dark Continent, Busch Gardens, Tampa, Florida, feed and care for a baby Grevy's zebra. When she is strong and big enough, she will be released to fend for herself among the herd on the park's African veldt.

sources. In some places, wildlife forms the basis of the tourist industry. Visitors to South Africa, Kenya, and other countries regularly journey by bus into the countryside to marvel at the untamed world. Game ranching, where private landowners protect wildlife on their property and permit tourists to photograph them for a fee, is becoming a widespread practice. A portion of this revenue is used to support conservation efforts.

Many zebras and other creatures have become dependent on protected reserves for their survival. This form of confinement also creates problems. Achieving a balance between the number of animals and the land's ability to support them is of paramount importance. Without this balance, some species could multiply to the extent that vegetation would be devoured faster than it could be renewed, reducing the region to a wasteland. The eventual result would be the death of all animals in the area from starvation.

In some countries, comprehensive records of fauna (animals) and flora (plants) are maintained. Zebras and the vegetation they eat are included in this inventory. The procedure for tracking the zebra population in a given area is relatively simple. Game wardens assigned to a particular reserve monitor the known births and deaths on a monthly basis. The results of these surveys are then compared to the approved population figure (carrying capacity) for the area, which is based on the amount of food, water, and land available.

When the total number of zebras exceeds the ability of a reserve to support them, a reduction must take place. This is accomplished in two ways: surplus animals are humanely destroyed (a process called culling) or they are captured and relocated to another reserve.

Capturing a zebra and moving it to another range takes a great deal of care and skill. Unfortunately, some tried and true methods of rounding up horses and donkeys are simply impracti-

A crowd watches as Chief Senge, the regional game warden of Singida, Tanzania, feeds a young zebra that was sent to the new Sadani Game Park in Bagamoyo, about fifty miles from Dar es Salaam.

cal. Zebras can easily outrun a rider on horseback, unless he has a very fast horse. A high-speed chase by a jeep or truck for a long period of time might cause death from stress. Once roped, a zebra has a tendency to kick violently and drag its captor across the savannah. If subjected to excessive nervous tension, it might thrash about and cripple itself.

Modern techniques, including the use of helicopters, spring nets, and tranquilizer guns, have reduced the amount of human contact significantly, while minimizing the risk of injury to man and beast.

The sight of a helicopter can bring out the stubborn streak in a zebra. Most refuse to move at first, but even the obstinate ones are eventually convinced by the whirling blades and engine noise. Gradually, zebras are herded toward concealed spring nets that pop up and surround them when they are in the right place. Then they are tranquilized, moved by truck to their new habitat, and released.

Amidst the expansion of civilization, zoos also provide refuge for zebras. Some people say this is a mixed blessing. While zebras face no danger from predators in captivity, life in a zoo can be monotonous. Furthermore, it is argued that zebras were meant to live on soft sod and grass, not asphalt or concrete. There are many who feel that exhibiting these freedom-loving creatures behind bars is cruel treatment. Fortunately, the current attitude toward zoo planning is to provide zebras and other wild animals with living space closely resembling their natural habitats.

Most zoos obtain their zebras through purchases from dealers who import animals from Africa or by mating their existing stock. Surplus zebras are sold to other zoos to replace those that have

Old photo shows zookeeper feeding zebras at the Whipsnade Zoo, England.

Zebras, the "horses of the sun"

died from disease or old age. Many of the offspring of zoo zebras have formed the basis of herds in game parks and wildlife reserves.

Caring for the wildlife of the world is a responsibility that zoological societies do not take lightly. Animals such as zebras are treated as prized possessions. Maintaining the health of a valuable or rare animal is very important. Most zebras receive a regular physical examination from a veterinarian. This often includes a tetanus shot to prevent infections and a stool check for worms. Any sign of illness is treated immediately.

Zebras kept in zoos generally have access to the outdoors all year round. The people who take care of these animals have noted that they prefer the outdoors to their heated and air-conditioned quarters, even in extremely hot or cold weather. Environmental conditions uncommon to their native Africa don't seem to bother them. The Cincinnati Zoo's zebras enjoy romping in the snow!

There are usually more mares than stallions in American zoos. Not only does this eliminate competition between males (which would present a serious problem if a fight were to break out in a confined area) but also it preserves the natural family structure. Having more mares also increases the chances of successful breeding in captivity.

Through the efforts of many dedicated and caring individuals, zebras will continue to have a place to live—for now. It would be foolish to think that their existence in the wild is not threatened. Some people say that zebras are determined to ensure their own survival—by not submitting to the forces of nature or the onslaught of man's civilization.

Index

Berkwagga, 27
Boehm's zebra. *See* Grant's zebra
Bontequagga, 21
Burchell, William John, 25
Burchell's zebra, 24–25

Cape mountain zebra, 28–29
Chapman's zebra, 21, 24
Cincinnati Zoo, 62
Common zebra. *See* Plains zebra

Damara. *See* Chapman's zebra
Darwin, Charles, 34

Equus burchelli, 9, 24–26
Equus grevyi, 10, 29
Equus quagga quagga, 25–27
Equus zebra, 10, 28–29

Grant's zebra, 24
Grévy, Jules, 30
Grevy's zebra, 10, 29–31

Hartmann's mountain zebra, 29
Hippotigris, 7
"Horse-tiger," 7
Hyracotherium, 11

Menelik I, 30
Miocene era, 11
Mountain zebra, 10, 27–29

Plains zebra, 9, 21, 24–27

Quagga, 25–27

Selous' zebra, 24

True zebra. *See* Mountain zebra

Zebra
　ancestors, 11
　characteristics, 7, 9, 21, 34–41
　in common speech, 19
　conservation, 57–62
　defense, 40–41, 50–52
　dewlap, 9, 27
　diet, 38
　domesticated, 31
　ears, 27, 30
　enemies, 50–53, 55–56
　in Equidae family, 9
　evolution, 11
　eyes, 37
　hoofs, 9, 11, 28, 37, 41

horse, comparison to, 7, 9, 21, 30, 34
in lore, 19
mane, 9
migration, 42
mouth, 13
muzzle, 21, 27
origin of the word, 17
personality, 41
reproduction, 46
running, 34–35, 59
social organization, 43–44

species, 9
stripes, 13–15, 17, 21, 24, 27, 30–31
tail, 21, 28
teeth, 11
terminology, 10
voice, 37–38
in the wild, 9–10, 42–44, 46–54

Zebroid, 32–33
Zeederberg Mail Coach Company, 31